Your Computer, Your ISP, Your Internet

I0482923

A.J. Rush

TABLE OF CONTENTS

Contents

Wireless Gateways, Hostility, And Setting Yourself Apart 6

Initial Setup For Any Wireless Gateway Or Cable Modem 8

Calling Up Your Internet Service Provider 10

Connecting Your Cable Modem To Your Router 12

Connecting Your Device Hardwired To The Internet......................... 13

Customizing Your Wi-Fi.. 14

Windows.. 14

Mac.. 15

Common Trouble Shooting Problems 19

First Time Connections:.. 19

Common Wifi Problems... 25

My Device Is On But I Cannot Get On The Internet Or On The Wi-Fi 25

Uncommon Troubleshooting Problems 28

Unable To Get On Specific Websites 28

Hardwired But Not Connected 29

Random Disconnects Over Wi-Fi 31

Random Disconnects While Hardlined 33

Unable To Surf To Any Website But Updates Are Still Possible ... 34

My Vpn Isn't Working Correctly 36

Yahoo (Or Other Email Provider) Mail Isn't Connecting On My Device! 37

Is My Tv A Smart Tv? 38

My Device Is Asking Me For A Pin To Get On Wi-Fi? What's My Pin? 39

My Device Is Slowing Down On Certain Sites, What Can I Do? 40

My Internet Is Just Not Working. 41

The Lights On My Wireless Gateway/ Cable Modem Are Flashing. 41

The Lights On My Wireless Gateway/ Cable Modem Are Flashing And I Cannot Get Online..42

My Samsung Device Won't Go On The Internet! 43

My Chrome Cast Won't Connect To The Network!..............................44

Rare Trouble Shooting Problems...45

Symptoms: Pop Ups While I Surf And Underlining Random Text. 45

Symptoms: My Computer Is Beeping Excessively At Me At Boot. 45

Symptoms: My Computer Keeps Giving Me The Blue Screen Of Death. 46

Symptoms: All Of My Programs Are Gone, It's Like It's A New Computer...46

Symptoms: I'm Getting Redirected All Over The Net From Whatever Site I Visit...46

Symptoms: My Computer Won't Boot...46

Symptoms: My Laptop/ Computer Is Hot To The Touch. 47

Symptoms: My Computer Is Slow... 47

Programs That Can And Will Help 48

Programs Within Windows: 48

Antivirus Programs:... 49

Anti Malware Programs: 49

Something For Peace Of Mind... 50

How To Protect Yourself:.. 51

Solutions For The Common Man Or Woman 52

My Wifi And Computer Info.. 54

Wireless Gateways, Hostility, and Setting yourself apart

First off, let me explain what a wireless gateway is. A wireless gateway is a combination device. It is a combination of a cable modem and a wireless router in one device. I have heard that it's ugly, that it's bulky, and that it's inefficient. Truth of the matter is that this usually comes from people who don't understand technology, who don't want to understand it, and because of being this way, they will call up their internet service provider and bitch and moan until they get some sort of discount or about twenty different technicians to set up their shit, because they're too lazy, and too stupid to fucking attempt to learn a damned thing about what they have.

Now you may be wondering why I have such hostility towards those few. Let me explain. Put yourself in the shoes of those poor techs. Most of them are in India. A customer calls in yelling and screaming because their Wi-Fi doesn't work, their computer doesn't work, or they were a fucking moron jacking it to a porn site and clicked on a fucking pop up for an update to their java, and ended up getting a virus. Now as a tech, you don't get to yell or scream back, you simply get two options, deal with it, or give them a warning then hang up. Most techs don't get the second option, and end up having some serious problems because of it. Before you question it, no, I'm an American. It's those few who call in ranting and raving thinking that it's the ISP's fault when it's actually their own and the problem has nothing to do with the ISP.

Now, we can get into what I have to say regarding you the reader. As you read this book, looking for answers, you have set yourself apart from those morons that do not. Congratulations on that. If this book doesn't seem to have the answer for you, feel free to Google your problem, as that always seems to provide a multitude of answers.

Initial Setup for Any Wireless Gateway or Cable Modem

This part is the easiest part of anything. People tend to pay anywhere between 40 and 150 bucks for this alone, and you don't need to. You can pick up a wireless gateway from your local ISP's Store, bring it home and set it up yourself. Once you have it home, follow these steps and you'll be set up and ready to move on to connecting your devices.

1. **Locate a cable outlet or line.** This will look like your common TV cord that goes into the back of your television.

2. **Unbox everything and lay it out on a table.** Take stock of what you were given. You should have 1 wireless gateway device, or cable modem. 1 power cord and 1 Ethernet cable. You may have also been provided with a cord to connect to the cable wall outlet. If you have these items you are ready to begin. If you are missing any of these items, go back to the store, and get what you are missing.

3. **Connect the Wireless Gateway or Cable modem to the cable line.** It screws in. Make sure it's nice and tight.

4. **Plug the Wireless Gateway or Cable modem into a power outlet.** I suggest using a surge protector, only due to the fact that ALL technology is very temperamental and a power surge can destroy it.

5. **Call up your ISP and very nicely, ask them to activate it.** The Activations are usually automated, but in the case of getting a human being, treat them like one. It'll get you a lot further then cursing them out.

Simple enough right? 5 steps. Once activated you should be able to get online. Most wireless gateways have 4 main lights. Power, US/DS, Online and Wi-Fi. Cable modems will have separate US and DS lights and a link light instead of a Wi-Fi light. While the Wireless Gateway or Modem is booting or being programed, the US/DS or the US and DS lights will blink. The Wi-Fi light will blink if you have a device on the Wi-Fi. The Link light on the modem will blink if an Ethernet cable is plugged into the cable modem.

Calling Up your Internet Service Provider

As I said in previous paragraphs, I have a real hatred for the people who call up and yell, or act like complete idiots when dealing with their ISP. Let me put it out there for you who don't get what happens. The technicians who are dealing with you are being paid to do so, HOWEVER, you are not their boss, you are not their mother, and you most certainly are not their wife. You are their customer. The customer may be always right, but the ISP reserves the right to refuse service for any reason. You being an asshole to them is included. My basic call to my ISP goes simply. I call them up. I ask for a "Provision", a "Factory Reset" or a "Power Cycle". These are industry terms. If none of those things work, and I could not solve the problem myself, I then ask for a "Trouble Call", also known as a "Service Call" and only if I cannot get out to their location myself, or I think the problem is in the wiring. Below are some things that you want to do on the call.

1. **Be polite** – Cursing, cussing, yelling, rudeness, and racism wouldn't be allowed in any business, why do you think that it would be allowed on the phones?

2. **Know what your issue is in plain and simple English** – "My Wi-Fi drops out at random, or my us/ds light has been blinking for an hour" is useful "Fix it" or "My internet is broke" are not. Think about your problem rationally.

3. **Try common troubleshooting steps before calling or be ready to** – Replacing what cables you can, splitters, power cycling the modem, or resetting it to its factory settings can save you a call, and time on the phone. Check out the section labeled: <u>SOLUTIONS FOR THE COMMON MAN or WOMAN</u>

4. **Be in a quiet room** – If the tech cannot hear you, the call will end quickly.

5. **Do not put the tech on hold** – Most call centers have a policy about being put on hold. So just don't do it.

6. **Don't question the tech's judgment –** You're calling them for help, why would you do this? Do you know how they're certified? Do you have their training?

7. **Do not put the tech on speakerphone without prior permission** – I can't tell you how much this hurts the situation more. Speaker phone makes it hard to hear you, and might get you hung up on.

Connecting your cable modem to your router

This is a simple process. Once you've unboxed and laid out your items, you can begin. If you have a wireless gateway, feel free to skip onto the next section.

1. Connect the Ethernet cable to the port on the back of your modem.

2. Connect the other end of the Ethernet cable to the odd port on your Router. This port will be labeled "Internet" or "Ethernet" and it will be alone. It will not be one of the ports marked 1, 2, 3 or 4.

3. Plug in the router.

4. Wait for it to boot up fully.

Connecting your Device hardwired to the internet

"Hardwiring" is simple. "Hardwire" is an industry term. It basically means that you've taken a wire and put it from your device to the Wireless gateway, router or modem. That wire is usually an Ethernet cable. Not all devices have the ability to connect in this fashion, but some do, and it tends to make for a faster connection to the internet.

Customizing your Wi-Fi

After connecting to the network through either the "hardwire" method, or using the defaults for the Wi-Fi, the next step is logging into the router or Wireless Gateway. So open up an internet browser window, and up where it says HTTP:// you're going to have to type an address. The address is usually printed on the router or the wireless gateway, or in the instruction manual that came with it. Failing that, you can always do the following:

WINDOWS

1. Press the windows (flag, or four square) key on your keyboard and the letter R at the same time.

2. Type cmd in the box that shows up and hit Okay or Enter

3. Type in: ipconfig

4. Write down what it says next to default gateway. Some ISPs will have it set to 10.0.0.1, others will have 192.168.0.1, routers you tend to buy will have 192.168.1.1, or 192.168.2.1. But write it down regardless.

MAC

1. Open a terminal window by typing "TERMINAL" into the finder bar at the top right of your screen.

2. Type in: ipconfig

3. Write down what it says next to default gateway. Some ISPs will have it set to 10.0.0.1, others will have 192.168.0.1, routers you tend to buy will have 192.168.1.1, or 192.168.2.1. But write it down regardless.

Note: if you don't get an IPv4 address (meaning 4 sets of numbers separated by periods) and instead get numbers separated by colons, call your ISP and ask them to "Provision" your modem or Wireless gateway. This tends to clear it up; in the case that it doesn't then the device is likely faulty and needs replacement.

Type the IPV4 address into the address bar where I told you to before, replacing anything after HTTP:// with it. This will bring you to a log in screen. Again, the logins should be printed on either the instructions that came with the router or wireless gateway, or they should be on the actual device. If neither is true, you can surf over to routerpasswords.com, they have a bunch listed and it's a good place to start guessing.

Note: If the default passwords do not get you in, it is more than likely you bought some refurbished piece of shit or at least were given one. Flip to the section labeled: SOLUTIONS FOR THE COMMON MAN or WOMAN in order to fix this issue.

After logging in to the router or wireless gateway, you will be prompted with some options in the form of a menu with links or tabs. The tabs or menu will be different depending on the make and model of the router or wireless gateway. This is the main reason your ISP will not support 3rd party equipment. Since it changes, a tech would have to know the ins and outs of each one without looking at it.

You'll want to find "Wireless" or "Wi-Fi" in the menu. Once this is found, click on it. In mine it's out in the open, but a friend who lives in the state of Washington, who has Comcast, has his hidden under "Connection". You may be given an edit button, which, in my opinion is redundant inside a router or wireless gateway. When they have the damned button, they don't show you anything but the Wi-Fi name and it's encryption, which is shit you could've fucking guessed at.

After getting inside the Wireless menu, you'll want to get your configuration over manual if it's not already there.

NOTE: WPS in my opinion, has always stood for "Worthless Piece of Shit", because if you're using it, you're more likely to get hacked by your neighbors or people you distrust. Trust me when I say "TURN IT OFF."

Now let's customize that network. Look around your house for devices. What do you have? Is it mainly MAC or APPLE devices? Or Do you have windows and Android stuff? I've included some sheets at the end of this book to help you in marking down what you have for future reference. You don't have to use the sheets, but they do come in handy.

First, let's choose a network name. Trust me when I say you do not want this at its default. There are two reasons for it. The first reason is that any device that already has the default network information in it will get confused and you, yes you, will have to remove the network saved on that device and then re-add it to clear up the problem, and the second is that it makes you a target for hackers, and those random school kids that hang around outside your house looking for free Wi-Fi. Make them walk to Starbucks or McDonalds if they want Wi-Fi, don't let yours be used without permission. We'll be discussing why in a later chapter.

NOTE: Before we go on, you might need to save changes, if you do, I hope and pray that this is the only device connected or it's connected through an Ethernet cable. If you're doing this on a tablet, I want you to stop right here. Close the window out. You cannot continue on a tablet if you have to save after every change. The tablet would have to reconnect for each change, and it gets way to difficult way to fast. Go rent a computer or borrow one to finish up if you don't have one.

The next thing that we'll want to change is the Wi-Fi password. This is where things get a little tricky. 8 characters, either letters or numbers need to be entered to replace your default password.

NOTE: Do not under any circumstance chose something easy to remember! No birthdays, No phone numbers, no social security numbers! You are just setting yourself up. You wanna make a password that's secure regardless of who you are, trust me. Try a pet's name along with a birthdate of a relative, or your favorite president's middle name along with the date you got married.

After this, you'll need to hit "Save" or "Save Settings" to save what you've done.

Congratulations, you've just customized your network. You can close out of the internet browser window. Let's move on to trouble shooting now.

Common Trouble shooting Problems

A lot of things that people face on a daily basis is considered to be common problems when it comes to the connection of devices to their Wi-Fi. This section will cover them.

First time connections:

"My (insert device name here) won't connect to my Wi-Fi! It has never connected to it before but everything else connects!" Yeah, usually this is a problem with range, network type or credentials.

Range

Normally, Wireless gateways don't have that good of range, especially since you most likely got it from your ISP. While getting one is not a bad idea, and can save you money in the short run, you have to remember that most of them have a range of under 50 feet. That's not a good range, no matter what way you look at it. You may be wondering why your ISP just bought these from a manufacturer and is now renting this shitty piece of equipment to you. To make money. That is the only answer. If you go into business, what do you want to do? Make money? Yeah that's the reason anyone goes into business. So what happens? Well, the head of the marketing department tells the head of the department that oversees the equipment that customers have dropped their opinion yet again, or the guy running the financials tells him that equipment is no longer being rented at a certain rate, and it's up to one man to find a company that can produce a Wireless Gateway that will fill the needs of the customer. Nothing too powerful, as something that advanced would cost a lot of money. Something that they could rent out, and if it went missing, it wouldn't be a huge loss.

Navigating over to Mydeviceinfo.comcast.net, which is the listing for Comcast compatible equipment, is a good place to show a good example. In the time this book was written, a Device can be found on this page with a red exclamation point. Clicking on to this device tells how a number of the "Cisco DPC3939" have been stolen and essentially sold on eBay. This is what happens when a good device is handed out to different areas by a company. The device in question is actually more powerful than the other wireless gateways that Comcast rents, being one of the few devices that can support the top speeds they offer for consumers, and has a dual band offering at both 2.4 and 5 Ghz.

Okay, so back to range, what can you do to fix it. You have 2 options here. Move the device closer to the Wireless Gateway or router, or extend the range. Range is gonna be an issue regardless, so since moving the device in question speaks for itself, let's talk range extensions. A range extender is a device that allows you to add range to your Wi-Fi network. Your ISP will not support extenders, but the Original Equipment Manufacturer, or OEM for short, will. Why is this important? Well let's look at the average two bedroom apartment. Its 1000 square feet. This is an average for an area I live in at current, and no specifics are being taken from it, it's just an example. The range may be covered by the wireless gateway, unless it's a faulty piece of shit, but the quality is going to drop in slow increments. Anything can drop the range through interference. I do mean anything when I say this. Objects, electrical or not can interfere with signal. Range extenders allow you to make the Wi-Fi extend further throughout your home.

Network Type

Okay, let's address the elephant in the room now. Network type. Nintendo Ds and DS lite and a Samsung Smart Television. These are my favorite two examples. Owning either one will cause you problems off the bat if you want it on Wi-Fi. There are alternate routes, but more than likely you don't want to buy an added piece of equipment or you are to fucking stubborn to realize that hardwiring a TV is a good idea if it's a smart TV. LET ME SAY THAT AGAIN. IF YOU OWN A SMART TV THE ONLY WAY YOU WILL GET OPTIMAL CONNECTIONS IS THROUGH HARDWIRING. Now that I've said that, I feel better. The older Nintendo Devices require a WEP connection, and Samsung Smart Tvs Require WPA2-TKIP only.

By now, you've probably called your ISP and OEM and have been juggled around a bit, or you've picked up this book with considerations of buying one of these devices.

Samsung

Well how do we solve it? It's simple. The Samsung needs a brand new network. So after you navigate back into your router or Wireless Gateway, we need to change something. The name, the password, the security type has to swap to WPA2 and the

Encryption to TKIP. No, you can't leave it on the "Both" option. It has to be these specifically. Save your settings and walk over to the TV. Manual connection Setup time! Below are the settings you'll want to dial in.

IP address: (Find your Default gateway address from earlier, and instead of .1 at the end, you'll want a .15 or a .30 at the end.

Subnet Mask: 255.255.255.0

Default Gateway: (Yeah you should know this, it's the address of the router)

DNS Server 1: 8.8.8.8

DNS Server 2: 8.8.4.4

The DNS Servers belong to Google. What's a DNS Server? When you plug in a word address into your browser such as Netflix.com; that's the address the device will call out to in order to ask "Where can I find this address?" Google seems to work really well, and never has a problem that I've seen with Samsung products.

And you're done! Congrats, you just saved yourself a call to your ISP.

Older Nintendo Products

Honestly, I'm just gonna say, there's no reason to want to connect these anymore. Nintendo has pretty much taken down the Pokémon servers for the older games but whatever. For the sake of argument, you'd need to set your Security mode to WEP for this. I like to do this with a throw away router that I've bought for 3 bucks from Good Will. Why? Because WEP is unbelievably insecure. Honestly, a 2DS or 3DS would probably be better for your kids at this point, mainly due to the fact that their older gaming systems can't play the newer shit, or it's not covered by warrantees anymore.

But anyways, navigate to your router, and log in. Hit the wireless page, and change the wifi name, password, and Security mode to WEP. Save settings and you're done.

Credentials

Let's move on to the most common of these problems. Credentials. "I'm getting authentication error when connecting to my Wi-Fi" Yeah, this usually happens when you're entering the password wrong, or connecting to the wrong network. If you just skipped to this section, head back to <u>Customizing your wifi</u> and follow the steps to log into your router. Log in and double check your password against what you've been entering.

Still getting the error? Move onto: <u>SOLUTIONS FOR THE COMMON MAN or WOMAN</u>.

COMMON WIFI PROBLEMS

My device is on but I cannot get on the internet or on the Wi-Fi

This can happen without you realizing it, it can seem like everything is fine. You can connect? Alright, great! Oh, wait, no, it's not fine. You still can't get out to the internet. Why? Well your device isn't working right! Yeah, no shit. No I don't mean your iPad. I mean your Wireless Gateway, Router or Modem. Head to the section labeled: <u>SOLUTIONS FOR THE COMMON MAN or WOMAN</u>.

I try to turn my power on my computer on but nothing happens.

You may need a specialist. Pull out your phone book, and find a repair shop. It's more than likely your computer is in a state of hardware failure. It could be many parts, and this book does not cover basic trouble shooting for each part.

I try to turn on my computer, nothing happens, and yes, there's a power outage going on.

You, sir or ma'am, are an idiot. Put down this book, take your computer and throw it out, then move to a cave somewhere. You don't deserve to enjoy the wonders of electricity.

My screen says "No Signal" then shuts off after a short period of time.

It's most likely that your screen is not getting a signal from your computer. Please verify that the cables are connected properly and working. If you cannot do so, consult a local repair technician.

My computer is making a lot of noise, it's a whirring sound!

This is caused by one or more of your fans working extra hard. The solution is simple. Go out and buy a can of dust spray and open up your computer. Spray thoroughly after making sure the computer is off. Take a vacuum and vacuum any leftover dust.

My computer is making a lot of noise, it's a clicking sound!

You, my poor friend, are in for a hit to the wallet. The clicking sound means that your Hard Disk Drive is about to die. You will either want to replace your Hard Disk drive or your entire computer.

Uncommon Troubleshooting Problems

Okay, this section will cover those uncommon problems. Believe it or not, this shit happens all the time, but rarely requires a call to your ISP. IF YOU GO INTO THIS CATEGORY YOU DO NOT NEED TO CALL YOUR ISP.

Unable to Get on specific Websites

The issue

This is not an ISP issue. This an IP issue. IP, or internet protocol. If you are unable to get on the site, but able to get on specific ones, such as chat roulette, or Godaddy or whatever, you are more than likely being IP Blocked. What does this mean? Someone who had your IP address prior to you was being an ass and got you blocked

How to Verify

Go to Google or Bing and type in: "Proxy". A website called "Hide my ass!" or "Proxy.org" should be in the results. You just need to click the link, fill in the web address and click Go. If it brings up the site, then it's an IP block.

How to Cure

There are TWO ways to cure this problem once and for all. The first one is the longest, but the best choice. Contact the site admin and find out why the IP you have has been blocked. You can identify your IP by typing "What's my IP" into Google or Bing. The second option is for you to call up your ISP to upgrade to a business account so that you can manually change your IPV4 address. It is expensive. There's a third option but it doesn't always work. Unplug your Modem/Wireless Gateway, and wait 3 days. 72 hours. Yes, I said that right. Plug it back in. You may have a new IPV4 address, but it's rare that this works.

Hardwired but not connected

The issue

This is not an ISP issue. This is a cabling or adapter issue. If you are calling your ISP, you should probably go live in a cave, because you're bat shit crazy.

How to Verify

Open up a web browser. Nothing? Okay, try a different one. Nothing? Okay, open up a terminal window or cmd prompt like shown in earlier examples. Type in: Ping Google.com; If you get anything else than reply from Google.com then you need to try to ping Google's ip. This can be found easily enough. Use a different computer to ping it, or just Google "What's Google's ip", or you can try any of the following address ranges to try to ping Google.

64.233.160.0 - 64.233.191.255, 66.102.0.0 - 66.102.15.255, 66.249.64.0 - 66.249.95.255, 72.14.192.0 - 72.14.255.255, 74.125.0.0 - 74.125.255.255, 209.85.128.0 - 209.85.255.255, 216.239.32.0 - 216.239.63.255

Again if you have anything other than "Reply from" then you have a cabling or adapter issue. If you get a Reply from then

it's a DNS issue, and you'll need to read: <u>Unable to Surf to any</u>
<u>website but updates are still possible</u>.

How to Cure

Replace the cabling first. Ethernet cables are cheap and
effective, but they're also easily worn out. After you've swapped
in and out cables, you'll know if it's just the cabling or the adapter.
If it's the adapter, you're better off just taking it to an A+ Certified
technician for a second look. It might just need a driver update,
which can easily be done by the technician, or it could need
replacement.

Random Disconnects over Wi-Fi

The issue

Okay, so what happens here is that your Wi-Fi, on your
device of course, will randomly disconnect during the day. This
issue is very simple to cure.

How to Verify

Check a "Hardline" device. Is it happening there too, or just on the Wi-Fi? If just on the Wi-Fi, then it's a Wi-Fi issue, head to the cure. If not, and it's happening on "Hardline" devices, then it's a line issue, and you'll need to contact your ISP to have a "trouble call" for line replacement.

How to Cure

Log into your router, and change the channel. A great tool to use is an Interference Analyzer, which is available on most devices in their store. You can find the channel with the least amount of users on it and switch to it. Otherwise you'll want 3, 6, 9 or 11. Those are usually the cleanest channels. If this does not work, you'll want to invest in a Wi-Fi Booster, which can be found at an electronics store or on Amazon.com. These things are fucking cheap for the most part, costing around 30 bucks. Trust me, the investment is worth it.

Random Disconnects while Hardlined

The issue

While surfing the net, you find that you have problems loading pages.

How to Verify

This can be caused by several things.

1. Your wires are bad, see: <u>Hardwired but not connected</u>
2. Your router, modem or Wireless gateway has gone bad, see: <u>SOLUTIONS FOR THE COMMON MAN or WOMAN</u>
3. The lines are bad, and you will have to call for a "trouble call" from your ISP, which will be addressed below.
4. Your wired adapter is bad and an A+ certified technican needs to look at your machine. Do this only after the "trouble call".

How to Cure

Okay, before calling your isp, let's see if it's an inside line or an outside line First replace the cabling going from the wall port to the Modem/Wireless gateway and power cycle the network. See: <u>SOLUTIONS FOR THE COMMON MAN or WOMAN</u> for instructions on doing so. If the issue is resolved then you're done. If it continues, change which wall port your cable line is going to. Again, Power cycle everything appropriately. If the issue is cured than it was the line or the wall port. If it continues call up your ISP for a "Trouble call" to find the source.

Unable to Surf to any website but updates are still possible

The issue

I can use specific programs, such as windows update, and my antivirus can update, but I cannot surf.

How to verify

Try updating your antivirus, or your Operating system. If it can talk with the update server, then your problem is this one. If you're unsure, open a terminal window, or a cmd prompt and Type in: Ping Google.com; If you get anything else than reply from

Google.com then you need to try to ping Google's ip. This can be found easily enough. Use a different computer to ping it, or just Google "What's Google's ip", or you can try any of the following address ranges to try to ping Google.

64.233.160.0 - 64.233.191.255, 66.102.0.0 - 66.102.15.255, 66.249.64.0 - 66.249.95.255, 72.14.192.0 - 72.14.255.255, 74.125.0.0 - 74.125.255.255, 209.85.128.0 - 209.85.255.255, 216.239.32.0 - 216.239.63.255

Again if you have anything other than "Reply from" then you have a cabling or adapter issue, see: Hardwired but not connected. If you get a Reply from then it's a DNS issue, and you're in the right place and head on down to How to Cure.

How to Cure

You'll need to change your DNS settings on the adapters on your machine. On a MAC or Apple computer this can be done in Network. In windows you will have to navigate to the network and sharing center and change it in the adapter settings. I always suggest 8.8.8.8 and 8.8.4.4 for alternate DNS servers from your ISP. Saving this new setting will solve your problems.

My VPN isn't working correctly

The issue

Okay, this tends to happen when your work uses Ip addresses that conflict with your Wireless gateway. This doesn't tend to apply to those with Modem router combos, and tends to happen more with those working with Comcast equipment. Specifically the 10.0.0.1 series for IP addresses and the Technicolor Wireless gateways.

Verifying

Well, check the router, does it have a sticker? Does it say Technicolor? Is Comcast your ISP? Is your VPN not connecting anyway, regardless?

How to Cure

First off, we want to identify your device. Phone, Computer, what have you, it needs to be identified.

Yahoo (or Other email provider) Mail isn't connecting on my Device!

The issue

Usually this happens when their services go down and has nothing to do with the ISP.

Verifying

Head to downrightnow.com and check if their down.

How to cure

If their services are having likely problems, then wait, if not, remove the account from your device's mail client and re-add it.

Is my TV a smart TV?

The Issue

You don't know if you bought a smart tv? Really? Okay. Fine.

Verifying

Google it.

How to cure

If you Google the model number and it comes up smart tv, there's your answer.

My device is asking me for a pin to get on Wi-Fi? What's my pin?

The Issue

You don't know your pin. Believe it or not, knowing it doesn't matter.

How to Cure

Your pin is located on the bottom of your wireless gateway. If it fails, you most likely have your WPS set up shut off. There is most likely an option which will allow you to enter the network key, it will have text above it that says "I do not have/know a/my pin."

My device is slowing down on certain sites, what can I do?

The issue

Slowdown on any or all sites.

Verifying

Check your speed through a speed test, if the speed test looks fine, move on to the issue at hand.

How to cure

Well this means that a few things could be wrong. Your computer could have a virus, or malware, which is worst case scenario. Your cache might need to be cleared which can be done in your internet settings, or you may just need to reboot your computer.

My internet is just not working.

The issue

> You need to be more specific.

The lights on my Wireless Gateway/ Cable modem are flashing.

The issue

> So you're bothered by the flashing light?

Verify

Well this one is a simple yes or no. The lights flashing can mean many things. It doesn't always mean something bad. You'll need to check if your internet is working. If it is, then there's no issue, and it's telling you something is in use. If it's not, check out: <u>The lights on my Wireless Gateway/ Cable Modem are flashing and I cannot get online.</u>

The lights on my Wireless Gateway/ Cable Modem are flashing and I cannot get online.

The issue

Well, this can be a real issue. If your lights are flashing and nothing is connecting to the internet it can be two basic things. Either your modem is booting up and you're a dumbass who can't wait for it to boot up, or you're not a dumb ass and there's an issue.

Verifying and Solving

Well from here we need to verify if you can get on or not. If it's booting up, we need to wait up to twenty minutes for it to boot up. Go make a pot of coffee and relax. Come back in just over 20 minutes. If it's still flashing and you cannot get online, contact your ISP for a replacement. If it is able to get online, then you're fine.

My Samsung Device won't go on the internet!

The issue

Samsung devices not connecting. This problem is almost too common for this list. But as a tech I only saw it once a day.

Verifying

Most likely you are able to get on the Wi-Fi but not connect to Netflix.

The Cure

Okay, into the router we go. Set up a new network with the Security of WPA2 and TKIP as the encryption. Then go to your Samsung TV and set up a manual connection with your router's IP address first 3 octets, 15 or 20 as your IP end, your subnet mask as 255.255.255.0, and your default gateway to whatever your router's IP address is. Sorry to just glaze over it, but I've stated all these things before. The DNS however is where you want to pay attention, and it needs to be set to 8.8.8.8, and that's it. If you want the full instructions check out the section above labeled: <u>Samsung</u>

My Chrome cast won't connect to the network!

The issue

Believe it or not, this means one of two things. Wi-Fi interference or a faulty chrome cast. Change your Wi-Fi channel as needed by following directions here: <u>Random Disconnects over Wi-Fi</u>

Rare Trouble Shooting problems

In most cases, any solution here is going to be "Take it to an A+ certified tech."

Symptoms: Pop ups while I surf and underlining random text.

Cause: You are infected with malicious software.

Solution: Either clean it yourself with a series of different Anti-malware and antivirus programs, or take it to a tech.

Symptoms: My computer is beeping excessively at me at boot.

Cause: Either your keyboard is stuck, or your computer's ram is not seated right.

Solution: Clean your keyboard and reseat your ram.

Symptoms: My computer keeps giving me the Blue Screen of Death.

> **Cause**: This can be several things.

> **Solution**: See a tech.

Symptoms: All of my programs are gone, it's like it's a new computer.

> **Cause**: Your computer has been reset to its factory settings.

> **Solution**: Reinstall whatever.

Symptoms: I'm getting redirected all over the net from whatever site I visit.

> **Cause**: Your computer is infected with malicious software.

> **Solution**: Either clean it yourself with a series of different Anti-malware and antivirus programs, or take it to a tech.

Symptoms: My computer won't boot.

> **Cause**: Could be anything.

Solution: Take it to a Tech. Honestly, it's not worth the time but you can be told easily if it's a power issue, a cord issue, or the thing is fried.

Symptoms: My laptop/ computer is hot to the touch.

Cause: Fan Malfunction

Solution: Tech.

Symptoms: My computer is slow.

Cause: Could be faulty hardware.

Solution: Tech.

Programs that can and will help

In the case, and it does come up, that you can't pay for an A+ Certified technician to come and help you out of a virus/malicious software program problem, the following programs can be used to help out. Do not use more than one Antivirus and Antimalware at any given time, as they can and will conflict with each other.

Programs within windows:

These programs, when launched can allow you to see what issues are happening on your computer and stop some things from running

Windows Defender – A built in antivirus/antispyware program within windows.

Msconfig – Allows you to stop programs from running or booting with your computer.

Eventvwr – Allows you to see what has been happening and what is failing.

Task Manager – Can help you to identify what is running. On a clean boot of windows, there will be anywhere from 29 to 50 processes running. If you have nothing running and this number is over 66, I'd be worried.

Antivirus Programs:

This list speaks for itself.

Avast!

Microsoft Security Essentials

Norton

McAfee

AVG

Anti Malware Programs:

Spybot Search and Destroy

MalwareBytes Anti Malware

Adaware

Something for Peace of Mind

Within the last few years, scammers have gotten more and more influential and dangerous. They will call up your home or cause a pop up on your machine, or even get you referred to them by people we'll call seeds. They will try to charge you hundreds of dollars for troubleshooting that this book has just listed off. Saying things like you're infected, or your internet is not secure, or even that you've been hacked.

If you get on the phone and they tell you to open up Eventvwr then tell you all the errors mean you've been hacked and infected, don't believe it.

If you get on the phone and they show you a cmd prompt then type in "Warrantee expired" don't believe it.

Frankly, if anyone is calling you, telling you your computer is compromised, I would question the validity of the call. Especially if they have a thick accent!

How to protect yourself:

Ask them for info they won't know! First ask them for the IP address of your computer, which you can find with a simple search on the internet. Next ask them for the make and model of the computer in question. Your ISP can see if it's windows or Mac, but the caller may not be able to. Next ask them for the CM Mac on your modem.

The last one is CRUCIAL! If they cannot identify the CM Mac of your Modem or Wireless Gateway, they're not with your ISP, and shouldn't be calling about problems with your computer.

Overall, never surf to Ammyy.com, Logmeinrescue123.com or Teamviewer.com unless you know and trust the person you are talking to. If you are that worried about your computer, thank them for their time, and get a hold of an A+ certified technician.

SOLUTIONS FOR THE COMMON MAN or WOMAN

Okay, so you're having some problems with your equipment. You have 3 basic options that will ultimately fix the issue.

1. Call your ISP. They usually have the solution and if you can get over the accent, you can get the problem solved.

2. Power Cycle – Unplug the equipment in this order Modem or Wireless Gateway, Router, Boosters/Extenders. Wait ONE FULL MINUTE. Plug back in everything back in the same order, waiting for each device to fully boot up before moving onto the next one.

3. FACTORY RESET – On the back of most Modems, routers and Wireless gateways, there is a button that you can only press with a toothpick or Paperclip. Press and hold it for one full minute. Don't count. Your counting sucks. No, seriously, fuck you your counting sucks, you have to use a fucking timer. ONE FULL MINUTE. NO LESS. Wait for the device to fully reboot, which can take up to 20 minutes from what I've seen.

4. Check your cabling – I should've made this number one. Remove any splitters from the equation. Swap cables. Do what you can to prove the cable going to your box is good.

MY WIFI AND COMPUTER INFO

DEFAULT SSID OR NETWORK NAME: _____

DEFAULT PASSWORD: _____

DEFAULT ROUTER LOGIN USERNAME: _____

DEFAULT ROUTER LOGIN PASSWORD: _____

CUSTOM SSID OR NETWORK NAME: _____

CUSTOM PASSOWRD: _____

COMPUTER TYPE: _____

OPERATING SYSTEM: _____